ELIZABETH I
& THE SPANISH ARMADA

Author
Colin Hynson
Consultant
Dr Richard Tames

ticktock
Reading Borough Council

THE CAST

Elizabeth I *Daughter of Henry VIII and Anne Boleyn born in 1533. Elizabeth did not make it to the throne until she was 25. As queen she steered England towards victory over the Spanish and economic stability. By the time of her death in 1603 she had won the respect and admiration of her people, and England was seen as a world power.*

Philip II *King of Spain and a strong Catholic. He hoped to unite his country with England by proposing to Elizabeth. She refused his hand in marriage and his attempts to convert her to Catholicism. In revenge, he built up a huge fleet of ships called the Armada, and tried to attack England.*

Sir Francis Drake *An adventurous explorer and pirate, Drake was a favourite of Elizabeth's. His exploits, which included robbing Spanish ships, brought him great fame. In 1580 Elizabeth knighted Drake as thanks for the wealth he'd brought to England.*

Duke of Medina Sidonia *Commander of the Spanish Armada. The Duke was in charge of one of the worst navy disasters experienced by the Spanish. He tried to conquer England with 138 ships and returned home two months later with about 70.*

Pope Sixtus V *Philip II of Spain convinced the head of the Catholic church to join with him against England. The pope was a powerful man with a lot of money. He declared a Catholic crusade against England. Shortly afterwards the Armada sailed to England, where it was defeated.*

Lord Howard of Effingham *A clever politician, Howard was very popular with Elizabeth. He was promoted from commander of her navy to Lord Lieutenant General of England. With Drake at his side he defeated the Spanish Armada.*

Copyright © ticktock Entertainment Ltd. 2006
First published in Great Britain in 2006 by ticktock Media Ltd.,
Unit 2, Orchard Business Centre, North Farm Road, Tunbridge Wells, Kent, TN2 3XF
ISBN 1 84696 004 5
Printed in China
A CIP catalogue record for this book is available from the British Library.

CONTENTS

ELIZABETH COMES TO POWER

In July 1553 the Catholic Queen Mary I came to the throne of England. She insisted that her subjects followed her religion, and Protestants were burnt for refusing to accept the Catholic faith.

Queen Mary married Philip II of Spain in 1554. It was meant to strengthen the Catholic faith in England.

Yes, but what will you do about Elizabeth? She may undo everything that you have created.

With you by my side we will take this country back to the true faith.

Mary died childless in 1558. The heir to the throne was her half-sister, Elizabeth. Elizabeth was not a Catholic but a Protestant.

Her Majesty is dying. You must fetch a priest to hear her last confession.

We must also tell Princess Elizabeth. She must prepare to become queen.

At first Elizabeth needed the advise of the most powerful noblemen in England.

Your Majesty, England needs stability. You must marry soon.

You must also keep the faith of the late Queen Mary.

Thank you, my lords, for your words of wisdom.

Elizabeth never married and she turned England into a Protestant country.

FAST FACT

Between 1555-1558 nearly 300 people were burnt at the stake in England.

In the 1580s Philip II controlled a vast Empire around the world.

NORTH AMERICA

ASIA

AFRICA

SOUTH AMERICA

Spain's Empire

With an army of just 500 men the Spanish explorer defeated the mighty Aztec Empire in Central America.

They have no armour and no swords. We can easily crush them.

How can we defeat these strange men and their weapons?

Hernan Cortes took Montezuma, the leader of the Aztecs hostage and demanded gold. The Aztecs rebelled and were defeated.

I demand all of the gold in your city. Then I will let you go.

You cannot hold me like this.

6

Aztec wealth poured out of Mexico and back to Spain. This new wealth helped make Spain the most powerful kingdom in Europe.

With all of this gold we will be able to defeat our Protestant enemies at home.

Yes and we will be rewarded as well.

FAST FACT Spanish treasure ships did not sail alone. They sailed in fleets of between 30 and 80 ships, twice a year.

ELIZABETH AND DRAKE

Elizabeth I watched the growing power of Spain with envy and fear. She wanted some of the wealth that Spain was gaining. In 1577 she summoned the sailor Francis Drake.

Mr Drake, I will pay for your ships to attack the Spanish but our agreement must be a secret. I cannot risk war with Spain.

Your Majesty, I will return to these shores laden with treasures for your glory.

Drake sailed to America and attacked the Spanish treasure ships.

These are easy pickings. The Spanish did not expect us to arrive.

We must continue our voyage and find new treasure for Her Majesty.

Philip II controlled a Protestant part of Europe now called the Netherlands. They wanted to be free of Spanish rule. In 1572 the people of the Netherlands begin to fight their Spanish masters.

The Dutch rebels fought hard but they needed help. They looked to the English Protestant Queen.

Elizabeth I sent the Earl of Leicester with an army to fight the Spanish.

Fight on! Drive the Spanish from this country.

In London Elizabeth I read an update about the rebellion.

If we can keep this rebellion going, then the Spanish will ignore my kingdom.

But in Madrid Philip II also read about the rebellion.

The cursed English. I must crush this Protestant Queen now.

FAST FACT The Dutch Revolt lasted from 1568 to 1648. It is sometimes called the 'Eighty Years War'.

Philip II began the planned invasion of England. He needed the help of the Pope Sixtus V. So he sent for his ambassdor to the Pope, Olivarez.

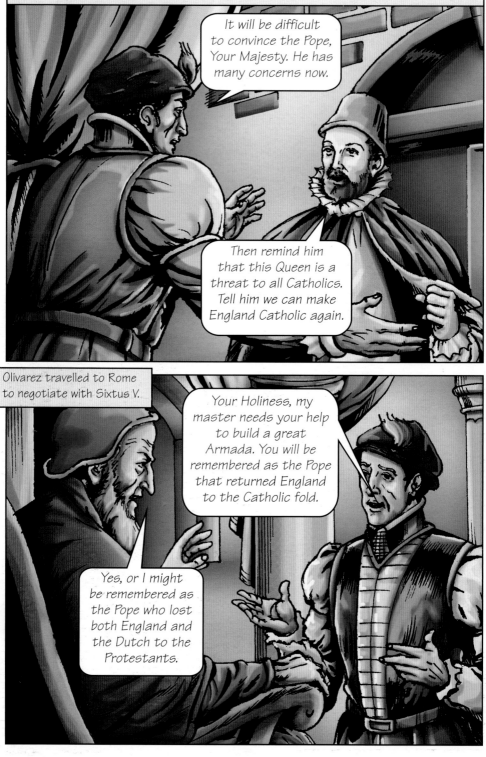

It will be difficult to convince the Pope, Your Majesty. He has many concerns now.

Then remind him that this Queen is a threat to all Catholics. Tell him we can make England Catholic again.

Olivarez travelled to Rome to negotiate with Sixtus V.

Your Holiness, my master needs your help to build a great Armada. You will be remembered as the Pope that returned England to the Catholic fold.

Yes, or I might be remembered as the Pope who lost both England and the Dutch to the Protestants.

Olivarez convinced Sixtus V by telling him that the English Catholics would rise up in rebellion (see below) once the Armada set sail. Olivarez was wrong. The English Catholics remained loyal to their Queen.

For our Spanish brothers.

For a Catholic England.

Down with the Protestant Queen.

Olivarez returned to Madrid.

My Lord, the Pope agrees to help pay for the Armada but only after we have overthrown Elizabeth.

FAST FACT While Sixtus V was Pope the dome at St. Peter's was completed and he had much of Rome rebuilt.

In 1561, Elizabeth I's cousin, Mary, returned to Scotland as Queen. She was a Catholic and she wanted to make Scotland Catholic again. She was also seen by many as the rightful Queen of England.

Your Majesty, your return to Scotland is most welcome.

I thank you, Father, and I pray that all of my people will join me in the true faith.

However, Scottish nobles did not want a Catholic Scotland and began to plot against her.

We must stop her. Will you join us and rise up against her?

She has married the Catholic Lord Darnley.

Although Mary managed to defeat this rebellion she was caught up in a plot to murder her husband. The Scottish nobles imprisoned the man she wanted to marry and in 1568 Mary was forced to seek protection from Elizabeth.

Mary found herself a prisoner of Elizabeth for nearly twenty years. Elizabeth knew that she was a threat to her throne but could not bring herself to execute a queen. It was only after a plot to assassinate Elizabeth was discovered in 1586 that Mary was tried and executed.

She was planning to kill our Queen. She must die to protect our country.

She is meeting her death like a true queen.

News of Mary's execution reached Madrid.

Your Majesty, the Queen of Scotland is dead. Murdered by Elizabeth.

Now we must ready the Armada to revenge her death and restore the Catholic faith in England.

I wonder what the Spanish will do now.

The English knew that they had to slow down the preparations of the huge Spanish ships (built to carry troops) so that the defences at home would be ready. In April 1587 Drake was sent to Cadiz for a surprise attack.

SPAIN

PORTUGAL

• Cadiz

The Spanish ships will be ready to sail to England soon.

Then we must make ready and stop them in their tracks.

The Spanish sailors had to take on barrels of fresh water as well as food and equipment for the voyage ahead.

Philip II commanded Admiral Santa Cruz to build the Armada at ports along the Spanish coast including Cadiz.

The English had begun to built a new kind of warship (inset). It was smaller, faster and better armed than the Spanish ships.

The English naval commander, Sir John Hawkins, was responsible for building the new ships for the Queen.

Your Majesty, I am honoured. But I get seasick easily.

Santa Cruz died in February 1588 before the Armada was ready. Philip II appointed Medina Sidonia to take his place. Sidonia did not want the job.

We will never defeat the Spanish with numbers of ships. We must rely on speed and agility.

The English cannons were more powerful than the Spanish. Drake could fire on them from a safe distance.

Steady lads! Wait until I give the order to fire.

The Spanish ships must be kept far away from us. Tell the men to keep their distance.

Drake destroyed nearly 40 of the great ships that were preparing for the Armada. He delayed the sailing of the Armada by a year.

Fire!

A hit! We've been hit!

Along with the ships the Spanish also lost valuable supplies including barrels of fresh water.

FAST FACT Drake captured and looted the San Felipe. This was one of the largest ships in the Spanish navy and it was loaded with gold, jewels and spices. The cargo was valued at £114,000 – a huge amount of money then.

THE ARMADA SETS SAIL

The Armada finally set sail in May 1588. It took two days for all of the ships to leave their ports. Medina Sidonia watched the ships sail away to sea. He was one of the last to leave.

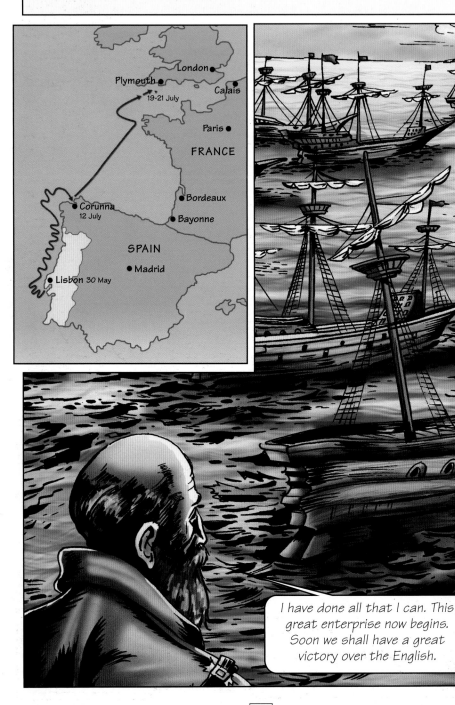

I have done all that I can. This great enterprise now begins. Soon we shall have a great victory over the English.

On the 21st July the English and Spanish ships fought their first skirmish. Little damage was done by either side. However, the Spanish suffered their first losses. Gunpowder on the San Salvador exploded and the ship was badly damaged.

Medina Sidonia had to decide what to do.

We must take the supplies from the San Salvador but leave the ship. It is too badly damaged.

On the same day the Rosario collided with another Spanish ship and was badly damaged. Again Sidonia had to leave this ship behind.

Let's make it the first Spanish ship to sail to the bottom of the sea.

The Rosario was a tempting target for Sir Francis Drake. He commanded some English ships to leave the fleet and attack.

The following morning Francis Drake and the crew of Revenge captured the crippled Rosario.

Now we can take the crew, plus 55,000 gold ducats on board.

FAST FACT The Rosario was one of the biggest ships in the Spanish Armada. It had 46 cannon and 300 soldiers.

On the 21st July the Spanish fleet managed to organise itself. It formed a giant crescent-shape over 7 miles in length. This made it very difficult for the English ships to attack.

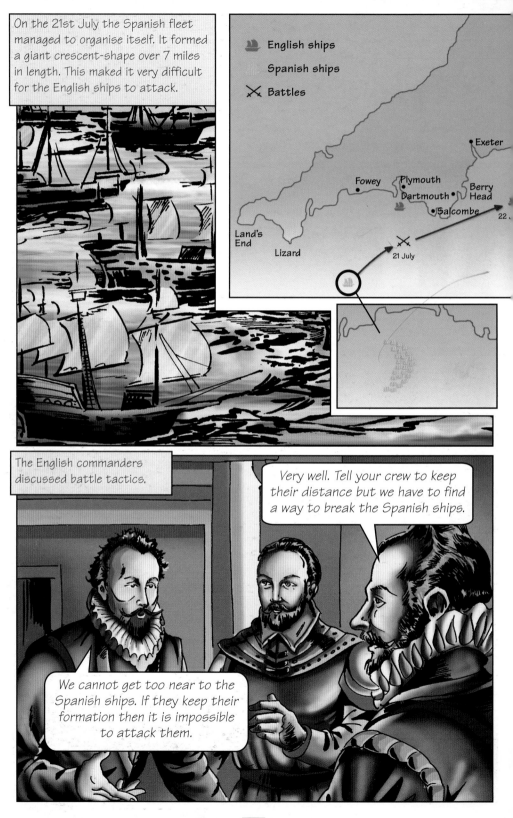

English ships

Spanish ships

Battles

Exeter

Fowey

Plymouth

Dartmouth

Berry Head

Salcombe

Land's End

Lizard

21 July

22

The English commanders discussed battle tactics.

Very well. Tell your crew to keep their distance but we have to find a way to break the Spanish ships.

We cannot get too near to the Spanish ships. If they keep their formation then it is impossible to attack them.

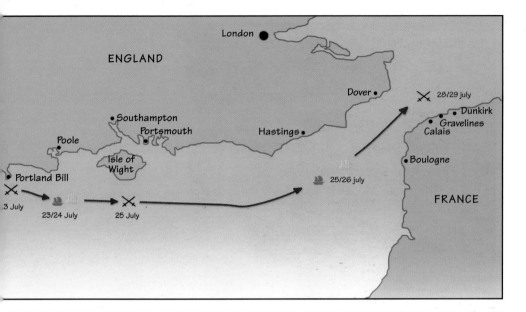

The Spanish and English ships skirmished at Portland Bill on the 23rd July. Then off the Isle of Wight two days later. Neither side made a breakthrough.

Remember lads. Keep your distance from those Spanish ships.

But we're too far away. We can't get a good hit at this distance.

FAST FACT The Spanish crescent was formed so that the strongest ships were on the outside and the weakest ships in the middle.

On the 26th July Medina Sidonia sent a message to the Duke of Parma who was waiting with Spanish troops in Flanders to be taken across to England.

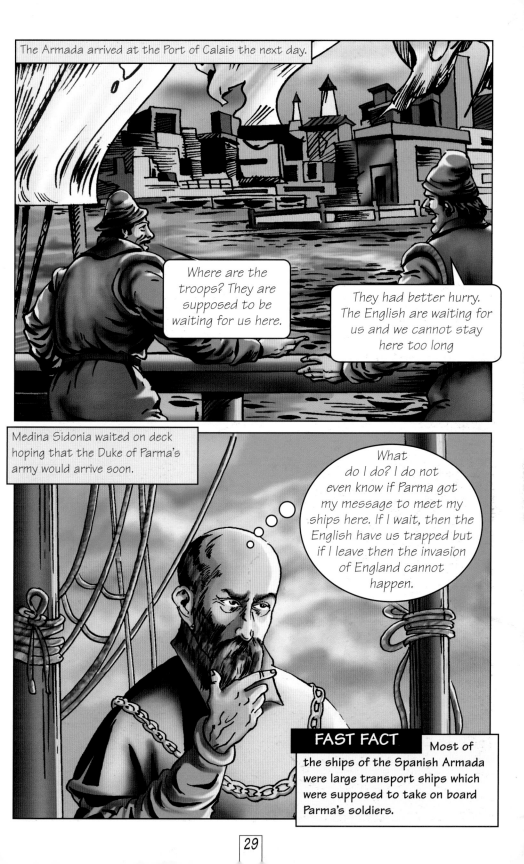

On July 28th the English commanders decided to send in the fireships. These were old ships that are set on fire and then sailed towards the enemy.

How many ships are we sending in?

Eight, my lad. The Spanish will panic and sail out of Calais and we will be waiting for them. All we need to do is fill these ships up with pitch and gunpowder.

The fireships were sent towards the Spanish ships. The Spanish reacted by using long hooks to try and push the ships away. At first they were successful.

The fireships were filled with gunpowder and cannon balls. The gunpowder exploded and the Spanish panicked. They sailed out of Calais in disarray.

Look out! It's heading straight for us. Raise the sails! Raise the sails!

FAST FACT   Both the English and Spanish used fireships. The Spanish used them to try and frighten off Drake during his raid on Cadiz.

THE BATTLE OF GRAVELINES

With the Armada out of Calais and the Spanish fleet scattered, the English commanders had to decide on their next move. Drake, Frobisher, Hawkins and Howard plotted together.

Shetland Isles

Orkneys

Hebrides

Forth of Firth

IRELAND

ENGLAND

London

Portland

Plymouth

Margate

Calais

Dunkirk

Gravelines

FRANCE

I agree. We should also split our fleet into four groups. It will make it easier to hunt the Spanish ships down.

Keeping our distance makes no difference. We must go in close and attack the Spanish at close quarters.

Howard

Hawkins

Very well then. Tomorrow we attack at last.

Drake

Frobisher

Supplies on the English ships were running dangerously low.

More English ships arrived and they were split into four groups.

There's not much left. How can we fight the Spanish without weapons?

Bring that ammunition up here lads.

Yes, my lord. Now they must listen to our entreaties.

You must take this message to England at once. All of our ships are short of cannon balls and shot. They must answer. I cannot fight the Spanish with empty guns.

Lord Howard was very worried about the lack of ammunition. He had already asked for extra supplies but all of his messages had been ignored.

FAST FACT The English fleet had 2000 cannons against the Spanish total of 1000.

The major battle of the Armada began on July 29th at Gravelines near the Dutch coast. The English ships sailed closer to the Armada. Their more powerful guns were now having an effect.

The Spanish ships tried to sail closer to the English ships so that they could board them and overpower them. They never managed it.

Aaargh!

Don't come any closer, you Spanish dogs. Otherwise you will taste English shot.

The wind is pushing us northwards. The English ships cannot be captured and we have lost several of our own. Without Parma's army we can do nothing. Order you ships to sail around this country and back to Spain.

Medina Sidonia decided that he could not win this battle. The Armada had to sail into the North Sea.

Truly this is a sad day for Spain.

FAST FACT The large Spanish ships used slaves as rowers. They were still very slow.

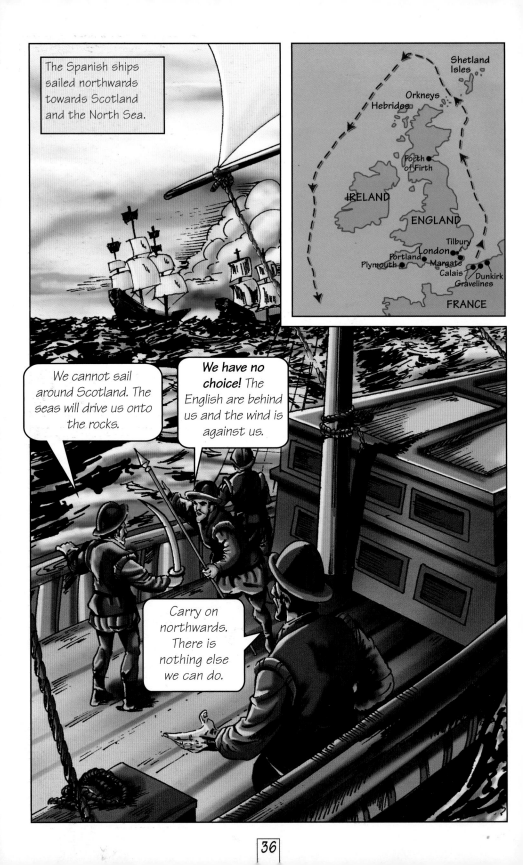

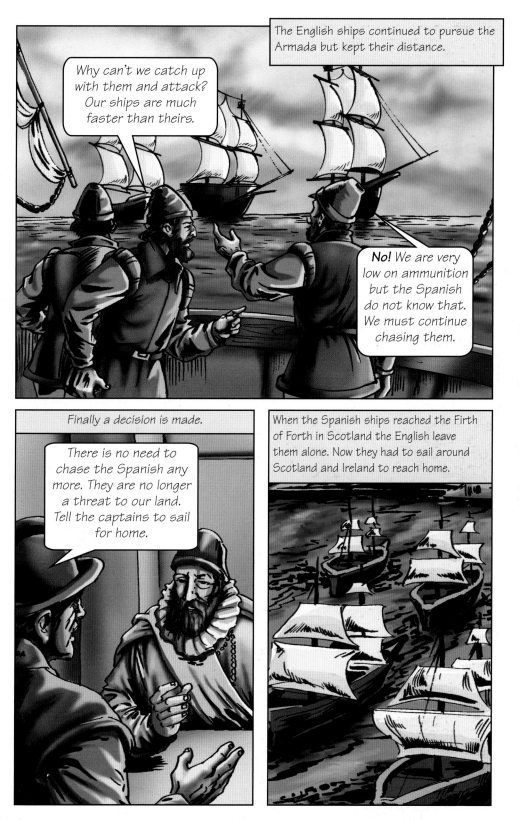

The English ships continued to pursue the Armada but kept their distance.

Why can't we catch up with them and attack? Our ships are much faster than theirs.

No! We are very low on ammunition but the Spanish do not know that. We must continue chasing them.

Finally a decision is made.

There is no need to chase the Spanish any more. They are no longer a threat to our land. Tell the captains to sail for home.

When the Spanish ships reached the Firth of Forth in Scotland the English leave them alone. Now they had to sail around Scotland and Ireland to reach home.

TOWARDS THE END

While the Spanish ships were being pushed towards Scotland, English troops at Tilbury waited for news. Despite being advised to stay in London for her own safety, Elizabeth insisted on meeting her troops.

Meanwhile, the Spanish sailors knew that not only had the Armada failed, but they faced new perils.

The English ships have stopped chasing us.

Yes, they have left us to the treacherous seas around Scotland and Ireland. We might not survive the voyage home.

Sidonia was warned about the stormy seas that they had to sail into. He was also told some more bad news.

My lord. The supplies are running low. We have precious little fresh water and not enough food to go around.

The men are already tired and dispirited. We must keep this from them for as long as possible.

40

41

Meanwhile, the Armada sailed into the Atlantic. Storms scattered the fleet and the Spanish crews were exhausted and hungry.

Nearly all the food and water is gone. What are we to eat and drink?

We should be enjoying the spoils of victory in London not fighting for our lives in this storm.

The Armada captains did not have any maps of the western Irish coast. This meant they did not know about the treacherous rocks that awaited them. Many ships were wrecked. Of the sailors who made it to shore, many were hunted down.

Run for your lives. I have heard that these Irish people show little mercy to foreigners.

Spaniards! Over there! Don't let them get away.

The battered remains of the Armada limped home on the 20th September.

Can those ships really be the same that sailed away nearly two months ago?

No, it is true. Our magnificent fleet have been defeated.

But we were told that victory was certain.

Medina Sidonia begged Philip II to be relieved of his command. Philip II allowed him to retire and refused to blame him for the failure of the Armada. The Spanish never seriously threatened England again.

FAST FACT

More than 1/3 of the Armada was lost at sea and over 20,000 Spanish sailors and soldiers lost their lives.

Elizabeth I, referred to by her subjects as the Virgin Queen, was one of the longest reigning monarchs of England. During the 45 years of her reign, she managed to transform England into a powerful nation with a substantial empire.

1556: *Philip II becomes King of Spain and the Netherlands*

1558: *Elizabeth I becomes Queen of England*

1562: *Elizabeth I contracts smallpox and nearly dies*

1564: *William Shakespeare born*

1565: *Tobacco first introduced to England; Lord Robert Darnley proclaimed King of Scotland and marries Mary*

1567: *Lord Darnley murdered*

1568: *Mary Queen of Scots flees to England in exile*

1577: *Francis Drake sails around the world*

1580: *Drake returns from his circumnavigation of the world*

1581: *Francis Drake knighted*

1583: *John Somerville attempts to assassinate Elizabeth I*

1584: *Walter Raleigh establishes a colony in Virginia*

1585: *Elizabeth sends an army to help the Dutch fight the Spanish*

February 1587: *The execution of Mary Queen of Scots*

April 1587: *Drake attacks Spanish ships at Cadiz*

May 1588: *The Spanish Armada sets sail from Lisbon in Portugal*

30. May 1588: *The Spanish Armada finally sets sail for England*

19. July 1588: *The Spanish Armada is sighted from the English coast*

21 July 1588: *The Armada enters the English Channel*

23. July 1588: *The two sides see action off Portland Bill*

25. July 1588: *The two sides see action off the Isle of Wight*

27. July 1588: *The Spanish Armada anchors off the port of Calais*

28. July 1588: *The English send in the fireships and the Armada is scattered*

29. July 1588: *The Battle of Gravelines*

30. July 1588: *The Armada begins to sail north*

9. August 1588: *Elizabeth I addresses her troops at Tilbury*

12. August 1588: *The English ships break off their chase of the Armada*

20. September 1588: *The Armada arrives back in Spain*

1590: *Sir Francis Walsingham, the queen's spymaster, dies*

1593: *Battle of Ballishannon*

1596: *Sir Francis Drake dies*

1601: *Elizabeth delivers her 'Golden Speech'*

1603: *Elizabeth I dies; James I crowned as first Stuart monarch*

1 There were three more Armadas launched by Spain against England after 1588. They sailed in 1596, 1597, 1599 and 1601. They all failed.

2 The first person to explore a sunken Spanish ship was Sidney Wignall. In 1968 he located and studied the Santa Maria de la Rosa.

3 One month after Mary I died and Elizabeth came to the English throne, Philip II proposed marriage to Elizabeth.

4 Philip II was a very religious man. He used to pray between three to four hours every single day.

5 Parma's army in the Netherlands was only about 18% Spanish. The rest were mostly either Germans or Italians.

6 The Spanish sailors were given a ration of one bottle of wine a day plus three pints of water – which had to be used for both drinking and cooking.

7 The Armada took enough wine to last six months. However, most of it was undrinkable.

8 Alongside all of the other ammunition, the Spanish Armada took 120,000 bullets with them ready for the invasion of England.

9 The men who had to look after the beacons that were lit when the Armada was sighted were not allowed to have chairs in case they sat down and fell asleep on duty.

10 At the start of 1588 Charles Howard, the commander of the English fleet, believed that the Spanish would land in Scotland and then invade England from the north.

11 The English sailors were given a gallon of beer a day to drink instead of water.

12 When Elizabeth spoke to her troops at Tilbury she was smiling so much that many people saw that she had black teeth.

13 On Sunday 4th December there was a special celebration at St. Paul's Cathedral to celebrate the English victory.

14 600 Spanish sailors were shipwrecked on the coast of Scotland. They were treated well and were returned to Spain.

15 Discipline on board both Spanish and English ships was harsh. Any sailor found guilty of murder was tied to the body of his victim and thrown overboard.

16 The first English person to sight the Spanish Armada was the captain of the Golden Hinde, Thomas Fleming.

17 The reason why the English ships did not have enough ammunition was they had quickly used up most of the materials available in England. The whole country nearly ran out of ammunition.

GLOSSARY

Armada: *A large group of ships used in battles in order to carry out strategic warfare (see also Formation)*

Barge: *Originally a large rowing boat used to tow large vessels out to sea. They were used by both sides to get their ships out of port.*

Beacon: *A way of communicating over long distances with the help of light or fire. Usually this signal represented a warning.*

Broadside: *When all of the guns on one side of the ship are fired at the same time.*

Bulwark: *The side of the highest part of a ship's deck.*

Catholic: *A member of the Roman Catholic church, e.g. King Philip II*

Circumnavigate: *A term to describe a vessel that travels around something. Francis Drake circumnavigated the world between 1577-1580.*

Coronation: *The ceremony in which a king or queen is crowned*

Draught: *The amount of water needed to float a ship.*

Decks: *The flooring of a ship. Most ships had more than one deck. These included the main deck and the upper deck.*

Execute: *To kill someone as a punishment for a severe crime. In Elizabethan times, the criminal was usually beheaded.*

Flagship: *The ship belonging to a navy's commander*

Fireships: *Old ships that were set alight and sailed towards an enemy fleet. Both the Spanish and the English used them.*

Formation: *When something is put into a particular order and shape.*

Frigate: *A small ship used by the Spanish to protect their treasure ships*

GLOSSARY

Galleon: *A large ship used by the Spanish with guns on the main and upper deck*

Hulk: *A large vessel that was intended to carry cargo for short distances. The Spanish Armada had them to carry troops over to England.*

Pope: *Head of the Roman Catholic Church, who was both very influential and extremely wealthy*

Protestant: *A Christian who belongs to the Protestant church, e.g. Queen Elizabeth I*

Race built galleons: *The name of the new fast ship designed by John Hawkins*

Skirmish: *An episode of irregular or spontaneous fighting*

Successor: *Somebody who follows another in a position - for example a monarch or a commander of a ship*

Smallpox: *A disease that causes chillls, high fever and pimples; if it isn't treated swiftly, it can lead to the death of the patient*

Stake: *A large wooden pole that was used in executions. Subjects who were opposed to the crown's religion were bound to it and burnt alive.*

Traitor: *Someone who betrays their friends or country. In Elizabethan times, a person who betrayed their country would most likely be executed (see Execute).*

Treaties: *A formal agreement between two countries*

Treasure ships: *Large ships used by the Spanish to bring gold and other valuables from Central and South America to Spain.*

Wreck: *When a ship is either destroyed or abandoned after hitting a rock or sailing into a storm.*

INDEX